for Isaac Stern

FIDDLER ON THE ROOF

Music by JERRY BOCK
Words by SHELDON HARNICK

Adaptation, arrangement,
and violin cadenzas by
JOHN WILLIAMS

VIOLIN

for Isaac Stern

FIDDLER ON THE ROOF

Music by JERRY BOCK
Words by SHELDON HARNICK

Adaptation, arrangement,
and violin cadenzas by
JOHN WILLIAMS

VIOLIN